Opposites

Big and Small

by Kelsey Jopp

www.focusreaders.com

Focus Readers is distributed by North Star Editions:
sales@northstareditions.com | 888-417-0195

Produced for Focus Readers by Red Line Editorial.

Photographs ©: Kellymmiller73/Shutterstock Images, cover, 1; Vixit/Shutterstock Images, 4, 16 (bottom left); photokup/Shutterstock Images, 7, 16 (top left); Paul S. Wolf/ Shutterstock Images, 9 (top), 16 (bottom right); Rudmer Zwerver/Shutterstock Images, 9 (bottom), 16 (top right); wassiliy-architect/Shutterstock Images, 11; Dimitris66/ iStockphoto, 13; szefei/Shutterstock Images, 15

Library of Congress Cataloging-in-Publication Data
Names: Jopp, Kelsey, 1993- author.
Title: Big and small / by Kelsey Jopp.
Description: Lake Elmo, MN : Focus Readers, [2019] | Series: Opposites
  | Audience: K to Grade 3. | Includes index.
Identifiers: LCCN 2018028261 (print) | LCCN 2018029303 (ebook) | ISBN
  9781641855174 (PDF) | ISBN 9781641854597 (e-book) | ISBN 9781641853439
  (hardcover : alk. paper) | ISBN 9781641854016 (pbk. : alk. paper)
Subjects: LCSH: Size perception--Juvenile literature. | Size
  judgment--Juvenile literature. | Polarity--Juvenile literature.
Classification: LCC BF299.S5 (ebook) | LCC BF299.S5 J67 2019 (print) | DDC
  153.7/52--dc23
LC record available at https://lccn.loc.gov/2018028261

Printed in the United States of America
Mankato, MN
October, 2018

About the Author

Kelsey Jopp is an editor, writer, and lifelong learner. She lives in Saint Paul, Minnesota, where she enjoys doing yoga and playing endless fetch with her sheltie, Teddy.

Table of Contents

Big 5

Small 6

Big and Small 8

Glossary 16

Index 16

Big

Some things are big.

Big things take up lots

of space.

Mountains are big.

Small

Some things are small.

Small things do not take up

much space.

Buttons are small.

7

Big and Small

Big and small

are opposites.

A **whale** is big.

A **mouse** is small.

This rock is big.

It is tall.

It is wide.

These rocks are small.

They are short.

They are thin.

Adults are big.

Babies are small.

They are opposites.

Glossary

buttons

mouse

mountains

whale

Index

A

adults, 14

B

babies, 14

M

mountains, 5

R

rock, 10, 12